What Can Live in the River?

John-Paul Wilkins

Heinemann
LIBRARY

Chicago, Illinois

© 2015 Heinemann Library
an imprint of Capstone Global Library, LLC
Chicago, Illinois

To contact Capstone Global Library please phone
800-747-4992, or visit our website www.capstonepub.com

Edited by Diyan Leake and Gina Kammer
Designed by Cynthia Akiyoshi
Picture research by Liz Alexander and Tracy Cummins
Production by Victoria Fitzgerald
Originated by Capstone Global Library Ltd
Printed and bound in China by Leo Paper Group

18 17 16 15 14
10 9 8 7 6 5 4 3 2 1

Library of Congress Cataloging-in-Publication Data
Cataloging-in-publication information is on file with the
Library of Congress.

ISBN 978-1-4846-0575-2 (hardcover)
ISBN 978-1-4846-0580-6 (eBook PDF)

Acknowledgments
Alamy: © AlamyCelebrity/Stefan Hetz Supplied by WENN.
com, 19, © Andre Seale, 9, 23f, © blickwinkel, 7, 11, 23a,
© Iain Cooper, 5, © Juniors Bildarchiv GmbH, 20, 23h,
© Malcolm Schuyl, 10, 23c, © WILDLIFE GmbH, 15,
23d; FLPA: © Terry Whittaker, 8; naturepl.com: © Daniel
Heuclin, 22, © Dave Watts, 16, © Jan Hamrsky, 21, © Rolf
Nussbaumer, 13; Shutterstock: almgren, 6, BMJ, 7 inset,
Bonnie Taylor Barry, 12, back cover right, Kletr, 18, 23e,
optimarc, 17, SurangaSL , 4, 23b, back cover left, tim elliott,
14, 23g; Superstock: Ron Erwin/All Canada Photos, front
cover

We would like to thank Michael Bright for his assistance in
the preparation of this book.

Contents

Some words are shown in bold, **like this**. You can find out what they mean by looking in the glossary.

What is a river habitat?

A **habitat** is a place where animals or plants live. A river is a habitat.

Habitats provide food and **shelter** for the things that live there.

A river is a large stream of water that flows across land.

Animals and plants have special features to live in rivers.

How do plants live in rivers?

Water lilies have roots at the bottom of the river to keep them from floating away.

Their leaves float on water so they can take in sunlight. Plants use sunlight to make food.

Bladderworts do not have any roots or leaves. They have small airless bags under water that help them catch food.

The bags trap tiny animals for the bladderworts to feed on.

Plants are very important for river **habitats**. They provide food and **shelter** for many animals.

Many plants provide a home for small animals.
These plants are called **microhabitats**.
A microhabitat is a very small habitat
within a larger habitat.

How do animals feed in rivers?

Crayfish eat plants and small animals.

The crayfish have large front **pincers** to grab and hold food. Smaller pincers on their legs help to tear away food and bring it to their mouths.

Catfish feed on plants, insects, and small fish. They live on the bottoms of rivers where it is hard to see.

Catfish have whiskers called **barbels** that help them taste food before they put it in their mouths.

Dragonflies feed on other insects. Their large eyes allow them to see in every direction.

A dragonfly's four wings help it to move quickly in the air. It can catch other flying insects.

Kingfishers feed on fish and insects.
Their long, narrow beaks help them dive
into water and catch fish.

How do animals hide in rivers?

Crocodiles are **predators**. They eat other animals for food.

A crocodile's eyes, ears, and nostrils are high on its head so it can sneak up on **prey** without being seen.

Freshwater mussels are food to
many animals.
Their green and brown shells help them to
hide from predators.

How do animals move around in rivers?

A platypus uses its webbed front feet to paddle through water.

Its flat tail helps it steer.

Pond skaters live on the surface of rivers.

Thick hairs on a pond skater's legs keep it from sinking into the water.

How do animals survive under water?

Most fish use their **gills** to breathe under water.

Many other animals hold their breath and return to the surface to breathe.

gills (inside)

Diving bell spiders have a special way of breathing under water.

They make a bubble out of their own web and fill it with air.

How do animal babies survive in rivers?

Beavers build nests out of twigs, branches, and leaves. They bite through wood with their large front teeth.

Beavers' nests, called lodges, provide safety and **shelter** for their young.

Caddisflies lay their eggs in water.

Some caddisfly babies make cases to protect their soft bodies as they grow.

That's amazing!

The alligator snapping turtle has a piece of flesh on its tongue that looks like a worm. Fish think it is food and swim right into its mouth.

Picture Glossary

 **barbels** pointy body parts around the mouth of some fish. Barbels are used to feel and taste food.

 **gills** body parts of a fish that help it breathe

 **habitat** a place where an animal or plant lives

 **microhabitat** a very small habitat within a larger habitat

 **pincers** large front claws that are used to hold things

 **predator** an animal that hunts other animals for food

 **prey** an animal that is hunted by other animals for food

 **shelter** a place that protects from danger or bad weather

Find Out More

Books

Ganeri, Anita. Exploring Rivers: A Benjamin Blog and His Inquisitive Dog Investigation. (Raintree 2014)

Waldron, Melanie. *Rivers.* (Raintree, 2013)

Websites

http://kids.nationalgeographic.co.uk/kids/animals/creaturefeature/
Under "Habitats," click "Freshwater" to see more pictures and information on river animals.

http://www.wildlifewatch.org.uk/explore-wildlife/habitats
Click "Freshwater and wet places" to search more plants and animals in river habitats.

Index